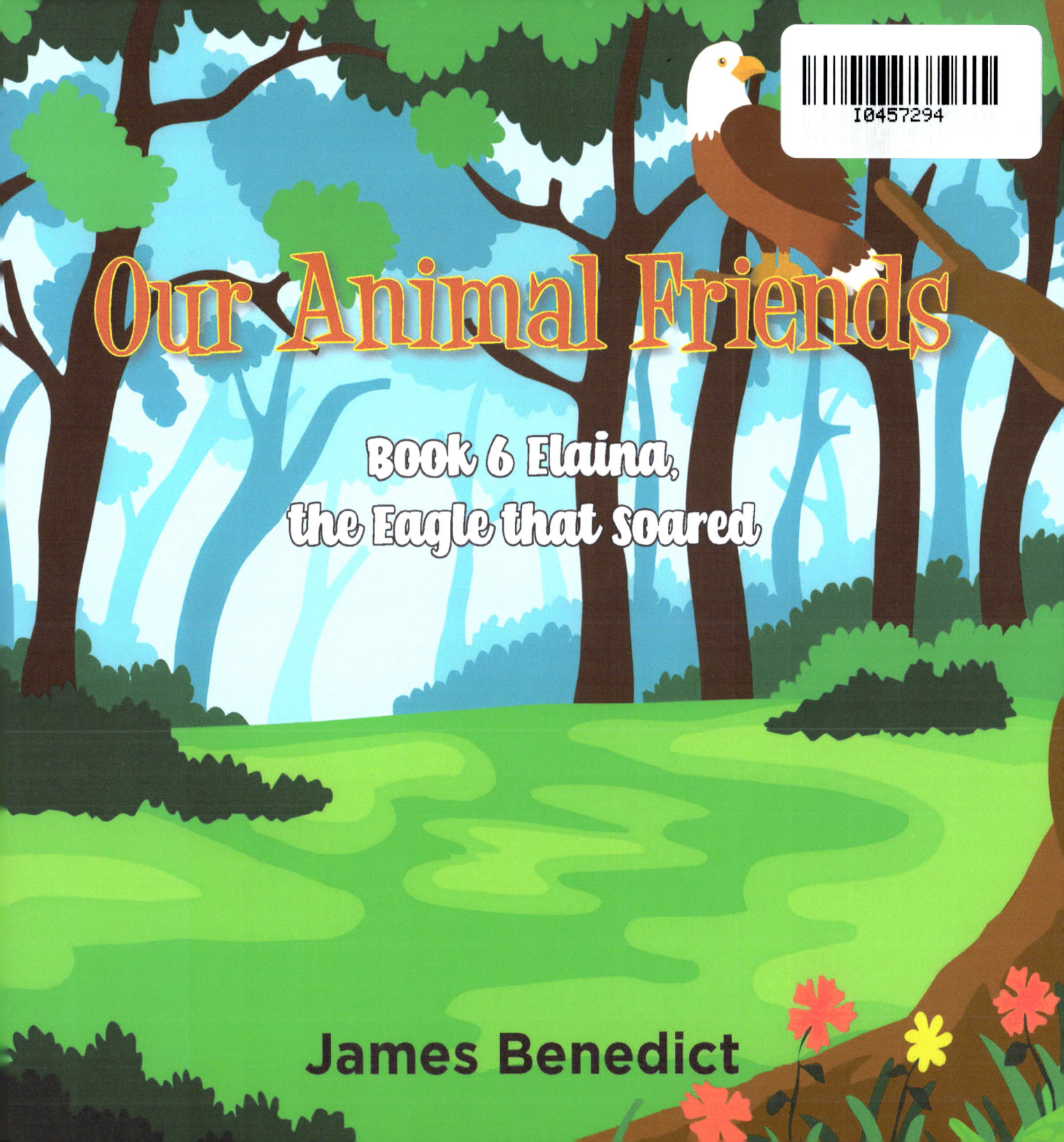

Our Animal Friends

Book 6 Elaina, the Eagle that Soared

James Benedict

THIS BOOK BELONGS TO:

_____

ISBN 978-1-959895-19-0 (paperback)
ISBN 978-1-959895-18-3 (ebook)

Printed in the United States of America

Everything is fine in the forest of plenty. The animals are happy but miss their new found friends from South America.

1

Sebastian, the wise owl, realizes just how his animal friends feel. Yes indeed, for he too misses their new South American friends.

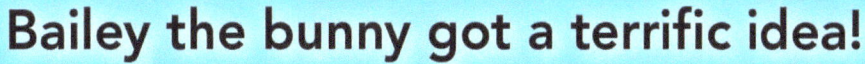

Bailey the bunny got a terrific idea!

Everybody was pleased and quite happy at the good suggestion! Then Sebastian made the recommendation to make a list, check it twice to make arrangements for the trip.

Hey, let us make a, "Bon Voyage," trip to visit all of our new found friends.

Does everyone know what it means to make a recommendation or to make an arrangement? Wow, they are big words that we need to learn what they mean.

A recommendation is a suggestion as to the best course of action to take.

Our parents make many good recommendations in our life for us.

An arrangement is a plan for a future event.

Our parents make arrangements to take us to school, church and the playground.

Arianna the Bluebird made a list of the important things to consider. Josh the fox from that list could make the travel arrangements.

Good Idea!

The list looked something like this:

Who was going on the trip?
Where were they going?
When would the trip take place?
What would they need to take?
How would they go?
And the very important why were they going?
Do you ever make a list of things to do?

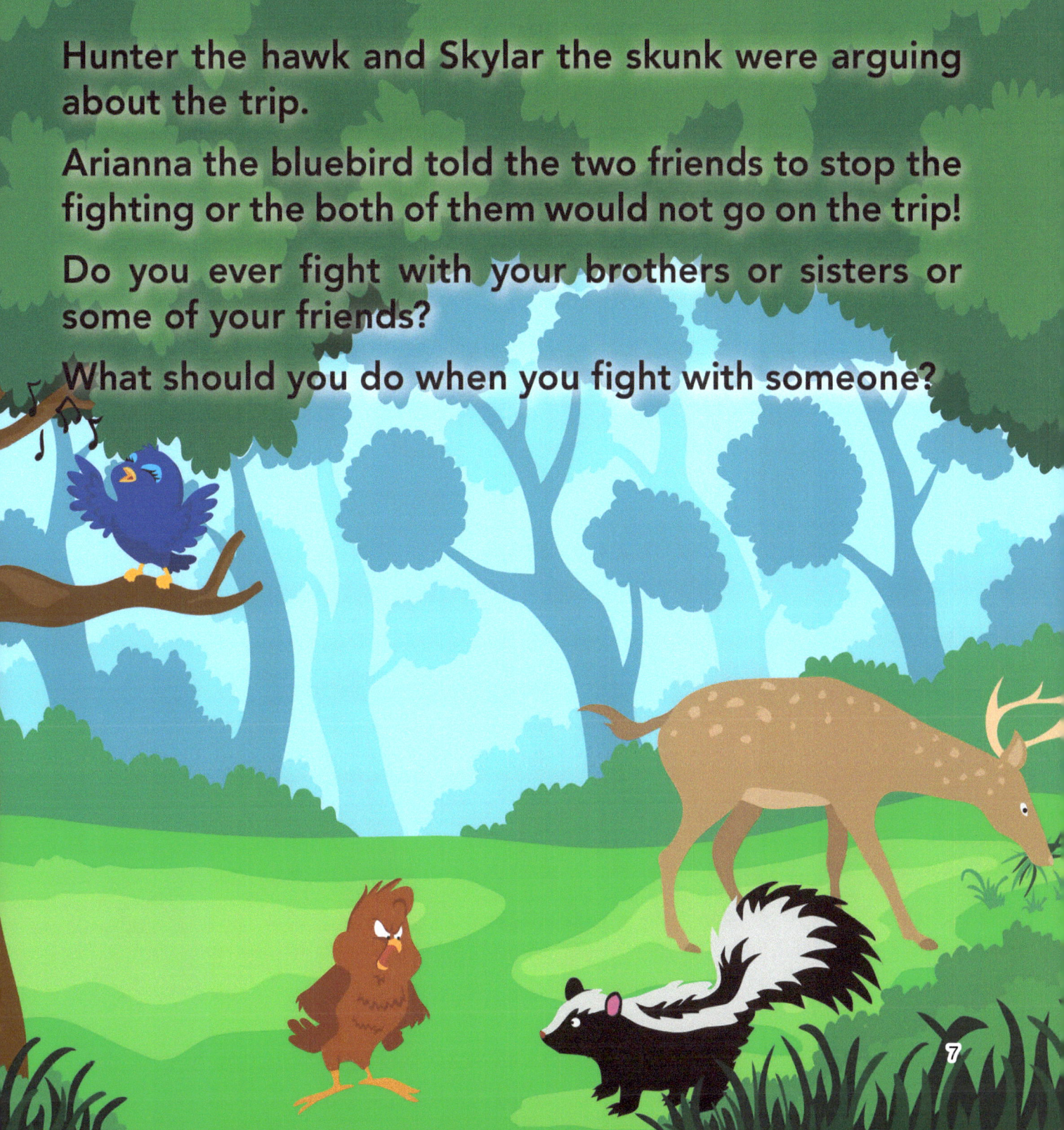

Hunter the hawk and Skylar the skunk were arguing about the trip.

Arianna the bluebird told the two friends to stop the fighting or the both of them would not go on the trip!

Do you ever fight with your brothers or sisters or some of your friends?

What should you do when you fight with someone?

peace is a beautiful virtue Every time we fight, each of us should say, "I am sorry!"

PEACE

We should always apologize for our bad behavior and always renew our friendships!

That is just what Hunter and Skylar did and they became friends again.

Guess what happened?

8

Hunter and Skylar were able to go on the Bon Voyage trip to Brazil in South America to visit all of their new found friends.

Do you know where Brazil is in South America?

9

Wow, look at all the countries in North and South America. And see all the beautiful colors.

The animal friends will travel from Miami, Florida to the port of Rio De Janerio in Brazil by steam ship.

Can you find Florida in the United States and Brazil in South America? Follow the arrows to find those places.

Great job! Hey, can you name the colors in Spanish? Let us try! Nombrar los colors.

UNITED STATES

GREENLAND (DEN.)

CANADA

UNITED STATES

Yellow	=	Amarillo
Orange	=	Anaranjado
Blue	=	Azul
White	=	Blanco
Golden	=	Dorado
Gray	=	Gris
Brown	=	Marron
Black	=	Negro
Purple	=	Purpura
Red	=	Rojo
Pink	=	Rosado
Green	=	Verde

MEXICO

THE BAHAMAS

CUBA

DOMINICAN REPUBLIC

HAITI

BELIZE

GUATEMALA
EL.SALVADOR

HONDURAS

NICARAGUA

TRINIDAD AND TOBAGO

COSTA RICA

PANAMA

VENEZUELA

GUYANA

SURINAME

FRENCH GUIANA

COLOMBIA

GALAPAGOS ISLANDS (ECUADOR)

ECUADOR

BRAZIL

PERU

BOLIVIA

PARAGUAY

URUGUAY

CHILE

ARGENTINA

FALKLAND ISLANDS

11

The ship was tossed about due to rough seas and all of the animal friends were afraid. But Sebastian the owl told all of his friends to be brave and the rough seas will pass. Sometimes life can be rough and tough but be brave buckaroo and the good times will come!

Skylar the skunk got sea sick and barfed on the deck of the ship.

The ship docked in Rio De Janeiro. Guess who was there to greet all of the animal friends?

Ricardo the rooster, Pauletta the porcupine, Giuseppe the guinea pig and Lana the Llama along with a new friend, Elaina, a beautiful eagle that soared high in the sky.

Brazil is a beautiful country! As all of the animal friends disembarked from the ship, they heard the sounds of music, singing and the sounds of, "Hola y Bienvenidos a nuestro hermoso pais!"

Which means, Hello and welcome to our beautiful country!

The following day all of the animal friends were invited to take a ride on the cable car to the summit of Pao de Acucar better known a Sugarloaf Mountain.

Rio de Janeiro is more than beaches and samba. There are many amazing hiking trails through the forest of Tijuca.

Ricardo the rooster recommended for all to take a hike through the forest.

15

Arianna the bluebird called for everyone to follow Ricardo the rooster. Ricardo led the hike through the forest of Tijuca. Pauletta the porcupine brought up the end of the line.

16

Sunset was approaching and Ricardo got very nervous that he took a wrong turn on the trail. Being afraid that he was lost is not a good feeling. Have you ever felt that you were lost?

Always let someone know where you are going!

Elaina the eagle soared high in the sky and could see that her animal friends were lost in the forest.

But eagles are the only animals that can look directly into the sun without being blinded. She got her bearings from the sun and flew down to show the way out of the forest.

All the animal friends made it safely back to the beaches of Rio De Janerio.

Thankful for their blessings, they all bowed to their Creator and made this prayer.

Thank you for the gift of life
Thank you for our safe return
Thank you for our daily bread
Please Keep us safe from harm
Amen.

It is the end of the journey for our animal friends. Old friendships were renewed and new one's were made.

As the ship got underway to sail our animal friends home, one could see Elaina waving and saying,

www.ingramcontent.com/pod-product-compliance
Lightning Source LLC
Chambersburg PA
CBHW041611120626
46551CB00002B/403

* 9 7 8 1 9 5 9 8 9 5 1 9 0 *